SISTER
MARY IGNATIUS
EXPLAINS IT ALL
FOR YOU

THE
ACTOR'S
NIGHTMARE

SISTER
MARY IGNATIUS
EXPLAINS IT ALL
FOR YOU

Two One-Act Plays by
CHRISTOPHER DURANG

THE
ACTOR'S
NIGHTMARE

Nelson Doubleday, Inc.
Garden City, New York

SISTER
MARY IGNATIUS
EXPLAINS IT ALL
FOR YOU

SISTER MARY IGNATIUS EXPLAINS IT ALL FOR YOU
was first presented by the Ensemble Studio Theatre, in New
York City, on a bill with one-act plays by David Mamet,
Marsha Norman, and Tennessee Williams, on December 14,
1979. The production was directed by Jerry Zaks; set design
by Brian Martin; light design by Marie Louise Moreto; costume design by Madeline Cohen. The cast was as follows:

SISTER MARY IGNATIUS	*Elizabeth Franz*
THOMAS	*Mark Stefan*
GARY SULLAVAN	*Gregory Grove*
DIANE SYMONDS	*Ann McDonough*
PHILOMENA ROSTOVITCH	*Prudence Wright Holmes*
ALOYSIUS BUSICCIO	*Don Marino*

SISTER MARY IGNATIUS EXPLAINS IT ALL FOR YOU
was then presented off-Broadway by Playwrights Horizons
in New York City, on a double bill with "The Actor's Nightmare" on October 14, 1981. The production was directed by
Jerry Zaks; set design by Karen Schulz; costume design by
William Ivey Long; lighting design by Paul Gallo; sound
design by Aural Fixation; production stage manager was
Esther Cohen. The cast was as follows:

SISTER MARY IGNATIUS	*Elizabeth Franz*
THOMAS	*Mark Stefan*
GARY SULLAVAN	*Timothy Landfield*
DIANE SYMONDS	*Polly Draper*
PHILOMENA ROSTOVITCH	*Mary Catherine Wright*
ALOYSIUS BENHEIM	*Jeff Brooks*

Characters

SISTER MARY IGNATIUS

THOMAS

GARY SULLAVAN

DIANE SYMONDS

PHILOMENA ROSTOVITCH

ALOYSIUS BENHEIM

Enter Sister Mary Ignatius, dressed in an old-fashioned nun's habit. The stage is fairly simple. There should be a lectern, a potted palm, a few chairs. There is also an easel, or some sort of stand, on which are several drawings made on cardboard; the only one we can see at the top of the play is either blank or is a simple cross. Sister looks at the audience until she has their attention, then smiles, albeit somewhat wearily. She then begins her lecture, addressing the audience directly.

SISTER. (*Crossing herself.*) In the name of the Father, and of the Son, and of the Holy Ghost, Amen. (*Shows the next drawing on the easel, which is a neat if childlike picture of the planet earth, the sun, and moon.*) First there is the earth. Near the earth is the sun, and also nearby is the moon. (*Goes to next picture which, split in three, shows the gates of heaven amid clouds; some sort of murky area of paths, or some other image that might suggest waiting, wandering, and a third area of people burning up in flames, with little devils with little pitchforks, poking them.*) Outside the universe, where we go after death, is heaven, hell, and purgatory. Heaven is where we live in eternal bliss with our Lord Jesus Christ. (*Bows her head.*) Hell is where we are eternally deprived of the presence of our Lord Jesus Christ (*Bows her head.*), and are thus miserable. This is the greatest agony of hell, but there are also unspeakable physical torments, which we shall nonetheless speak of later. Purgatory is the middle area where we go after death to suffer if we have not been perfect in our lives and are thus not ready for heaven, or if we have not received the sacraments and made a good confession to a priest right before our death. Purgatory, depending on our sins, can go on for a very, *very* long time and is fairly unpleasant. Though we do not yet know whether there is any physical torment in purgatory, we do know that there is much psychological torment because we are being delayed from being in the presence of our Lord Jesus Christ. (*Bows her head.*) For those non-Catholics present, I bow my head to show respect for our Saviour when I say His Name. Our Lord Jesus Christ.

(*Bows head.*) Our Lord Jesus Christ. (*Bows head.*) Our Lord Jesus Christ. (*Bows head.*) You can expect to be in purgatory for anywhere from 300 years to 700 billion years. This may sound like forever, but don't forget in terms of eternity 700 billion years *does* come to an end. All things come to an end except our Lord Jesus Christ. (*Bows head. Points to the drawing again, reviewing her point.*) Heaven, hell, purgatory. (*Smiles. Goes to the next drawing which, like that of purgatory, is of a murky area, perhaps with a prison-like fence, and which has unhappy baby-like creatures floating about in it.*) There is also limbo, which is where unbaptized babies were sent for eternity before the Ecumenical Council and Pope John XXIII. The unbaptized babies sent to limbo never leave limbo and so never get to heaven. *Now* unbaptized babies are sent straight to purgatory where, presumably, someone baptizes them and then they are sent on to heaven. The unbaptized babies who died before the Ecumenical Council, however, remain in limbo and will never be admitted to heaven. Limbo is not all that unpleasant, it's just that it isn't heaven and you never leave there. I want to be very clear about the Immaculate Conception. It does not mean that the Blessed Mother gave birth to Christ without the prior unpleasantness of physical intimacy. That is true but is not called the Immaculate Conception; that is called the Virgin Birth. The Immaculate Conception means that the Blessed Mother was herself born without original sin. Everyone makes this error, it makes me lose my patience. That Mary's conception was immaculate is an infallible statement. A lot of fault-finding non-Catholics run around saying that Catholics believe that the Pope is infallible whenever he speaks. This is untrue. The Pope is infallible only on certain occasions, when he speaks "ex cathedra," which is Latin for "out of the cathedral." When he speaks ex cathedra, we must accept what he says at that moment as dogma, or risk hell fire; or, now that things are becoming more liberal, many, many years in purgatory. I would now like a glass of water. Thomas. (*Enter Thomas dressed as parochial school boy with tie and blazer. It would be nice if he could look age 7.*) This is Thomas, he is seven years old and in the second grade of Our Lady of Perpetual Sorrow School. Seven is the age of reason, so now that Thomas has turned seven he is capable of choosing to commit sin or not to commit sin, and God will hold him accountable for whatever he does. Isn't that so, Thomas?

THOMAS. Yes, Sister.

SISTER. Before we turn seven, God tends to pay no attention to the bad things we do because He knows we can know no better. Once we turn seven, He feels we are capable of knowing. Thomas, who made you?

THOMAS. God made me.

SISTER. Why did God make you?

THOMAS. God made me to show forth His goodness and share with us His happiness.

SISTER. What is the sixth commandment?

THOMAS. The sixth commandment is thou shalt not commit adultery.

SISTER. What is forbidden by the sixth commandment?

THOMAS. The sixth commandment forbids all impurities in thought, word or deed, whether alone or with others.

SISTER. That's correct, Thomas. (*Gives him a cookie.*) Thomas has a lovely soprano voice which the Church used to preserve by creating castrati. Thomas unfortunately will lose his soprano voice in a few years and will receive facial hair and psychological difficulties in its place. To me, it is not a worthwhile exchange. You may go now, Thomas. What is the fourth commandment?

THOMAS. The fourth commandment is honor thy mother and thy father.

SISTER. Very good. (*Gives him a cookie. He exits.*) Sometimes in the mornings I look at all the children lining up in front of school, and I'm overwhelmed by a sense of sadness and exhaustion thinking of all the pain and suffering and personal unhappiness they're going to face in their lives. (*Looks sad, eats a cookie.*) But can their suffering compare with Christ's on the cross? Let us think of Christ on the cross for a moment. Try to feel the nails ripping through His hands and feet. Some experts say that the nails actually went through His wrists, which was better for keeping Him up on the cross, though of course most of the statues have the nails going right through His palms. Imagine those nails being driven through: pound, pound, pound, rip, rip, rip. Think of the crown of thorns eating into His skull, and the sense of infection that He must have felt in His brain and near His eyes. Imagine blood from His brain spurting forth through His eyes, imagine His vision squinting through a veil of red liquid. Imagine these things, and then just *dare* to feel sorry for the children lining up outside of school. We dare not; His suffering was greater than ours. He died for our sins! Yours and mine. We put Him up there, you did, all you people sitting out there. He loved us so much that He came all the way down to earth just so He could be nailed painfully to a cross and hang there for 3 hours. Who else has loved us as much as that? I come from a large family. My father was big and ugly, my mother had a nasty disposition and didn't like me. There were 26 of us. It took 3 hours just to wash the dishes, but Christ hung on that cross for 3 hours and *He* never complained. We lived in a small, ugly house, and I shared a room with all my sisters. My father would bring home drunken bums off the street, and let them stay in the same room as himself and my mother. "Whatever you do to the least of these, you do also to Me," Christ said. Sometimes these bums would make my mother hysterical, and we'd have to throw water on her. Thomas, could I have some more water please? And some chocolates? (*Enter Thomas.*) Who made you?

THOMAS. God made me.

SISTER. What is the 9th commandment?

THOMAS. The 9th commandment is thou shalt not covet thy neighbor's wife.

SISTER. What is forbidden by the 9th commandment?

THOMAS. The 9th commandment forbids all indecency in thought, word and deed, whether alone or with thy neighbor's wife.

SISTER. Thank you. Go away again. (*He exits.*) Bring the little children unto me, Our Lord said. I don't remember in reference to what. I have your questions here on little file cards. (*Reads.*) If God is all powerful, why does He allow evil in the world? (*Goes to next card with no reaction. Reads.*) Tell us some more about your family. (*Smiles.*) We said grace before every meal. My mother was a terrible cook. She used to boil chopped meat. She hated little children, but they couldn't use birth control. Let me explain this one more time. Birth control is wrong because God, whatever you may think about the wisdom involved, created sex for the purpose of procreation, *not* recreation. Everything in this world has a purpose. We eat food to feed our bodies. We don't eat and then make ourselves throw up immediately afterward, do we? So it should be with sex. Either it is done for its proper purpose, or it is just so much throwing up, morally speaking. Next question. (*Reads.*) Do nuns go to the bathroom? Yes. (*Reads.*) Was Jesus effeminate? Yes. (*Reads.*) I have a brain tumor and am afraid of dying. What should I do? Now I thought I had explained what happens after death to you already. There is heaven, hell and purgatory. What's the problem? Oh ye of little faith, Christ said to someone. All right. As any seven year old knows, there are two kinds of sin: mortal sin and venial sin. Venial sin is the less serious kind, like if you tell a small lie to your parents, or when you take the Lord's name in vain when you break your thumb with a hammer, or when you kick a barking dog. If you die with any venial sins on your conscience, no matter how many of them there are, you can eventually work it all out in purgatory. However—mortal sin, on the other hand, is the most serious kind of sin you can do—murder, sex outside of marriage, hijacking a plane, masturbation—and if you die with any of these sins on your soul, even just one, you will go straight to hell and burn for all of eternity. Now to rid yourself of mortal sin, you must go make a good confession and vow never to do it again. If, as many of you know, you are on your way to confession to confess a mortal sin and you are struck by a car or bus before you get there, God may forgive you without confession if before you die you manage to say a good act of contrition. If you die instantaneously and are unable to say a good act of contrition, you will go straight to hell. Thomas, come read this partial list of those who are going to burn in hell. (*Enter Thomas.*)

THOMAS. (*Reads.*) Christine Keeler, Roman Polanski, Zsa Zsa Gabor, the editors of *After Dark* magazine, Linda Lovelace, Georgina Spelvin, Big John Holmes, Brooke Shields, David Bowie, Mick Jagger, Patty Hearst, Betty Comden, Adolph Green.

SISTER. This is just a partial list. It is added to constantly. Thomas, how can we best keep from going to hell?

THOMAS. By not committing a mortal sin, by keeping close to the sacraments, especially going to confession and receiving communion, and by obeying our parents. (*She gives him a cookie.*)

SISTER. Good boy. Do you love our Lord, Thomas?

THOMAS. Yes, Sister.

SISTER. How much?

THOMAS. This much. (*Holds arms out wide.*)

SISTER. Well, that's very nice, but Christ loves us an infinite amount. How do we know that, Thomas?

THOMAS. Because you tell us.

SISTER. That's right. And by His actions. He died on the cross for us to make up for our sins. Wasn't that nice of Him?

THOMAS. Very nice.

SISTER. And shouldn't we be grateful?

THOMAS. Yes we should.

SISTER. That's right, we should. (*Gives him a cookie.*) How do you spell cookie?

THOMAS. C-o-o-k-i-e.

SISTER. Very good. (*Gives him a cookie.*) Mary has had an argument with her parents and has shot and killed them. Is that a venial sin or a mortal sin?

THOMAS. That's a mortal sin.

SISTER. If she dies with this mortal sin on her soul, will she go to heaven or to hell?

THOMAS. She will go to hell.

SISTER. Very good. How do you spell ecumenical?

THOMAS. (*Sounding it out.*) Eck—e-c-k; you—u; men—m-e-n; ical—i-c-k-l-e.

SISTER. Very good. (*Gives him a cookie.*) What's 2 plus 2?

THOMAS. Four.

SISTER. What's one and one and one and one and one and one and one and one and one?

THOMAS. Nine.

SISTER. Very good. (*Gives him a cookie.*) Because she is afraid to show her parents her bad report card, Susan goes to the top of a tall building and jumps off. Is this a venial sin or a mortal sin?

THOMAS. Mortal sin.

SISTER. And where will she go?

THOMAS. Hell.

SISTER. Sit on my lap. (*He does.*) Would you like to keep your pretty soprano voice forever?

THOMAS. Yes, Sister.

SISTER. Well, we'll see what we can do about it. (*Sings.*)
Cookies in the morning, cookies in the evening,
Cookies in the summertime,
Be my little cookie,
And love me all the time.
God, I've done so much talking, I've got to rest. Here, you
take care of some of these questions, Thomas, and I'll sleep
a little. (*To audience.*) I'll just be a minute. (*Closes her
eyes, he looks at cards.*)

THOMAS. (*Reads.*) How do we know there is a God? We
know that there is a God because the Church tells us so.
And also because everything has a primary cause. Dinner is
put on the table because the primary cause, our mother, has
put it in the oven and cooked it. (*Reads.*) If God is all powerful, why does He allow evil? (*Skips that one; next one.*)
What does God look like? God looks like an old man, a
young man, and a small white dove.

SISTER. I'll take the next one. (*Reads.*) Are you ever sorry
you became a nun? I am never sorry I became a nun.
(*Reads.*) It used to be a mortal sin to eat meat on Fridays,
and now it isn't. Does that mean that people who ate meat
on Fridays back when it was a sin are in hell? Or what?
People who ate meat on Fridays back when it was a mortal
sin are indeed in hell if they did not confess the sin before
they died. If they confessed it, they are not in hell, unless
they did not confess some other mortal sin they committed.
People who would eat meat on Fridays back in the 50s
tended to be the sort who would commit other mortal sins,
so on a guess, I bet many of them *are* in hell for other sins,
even if they did confess the eating of meat. (*Reads.*) What
exactly went on in Sodom? (*Irritated.*) Who asked me this
question? (*Reads.*) I am an Aries. Is it a sin to follow your
horoscope? It is a sin to follow your horoscope because only
God knows the future and He won't tell us. Also, we can tell
that horoscopes are false because according to astrology
Christ would be a Capricorn, and Capricorn people are cold,
ambitious and attracted to Scorpio and Virgo, and we know
that Christ was warm, loving, and not attracted to anybody.

Give *me* a cookie, Thomas. (*He does.*) I'm going to talk about Sodom a bit. Thomas, please leave the stage. (*He does.*) To answer your question, Sodom is where they committed acts of homosexuality and bestiality in the Old Testament, and God, infuriated by this, destroyed them all in one fell swoop. Modern day Sodoms are New York City, San Francisco, Amsterdam, Los Angeles . . . well, basically anywhere where the population is over 50,000. The only reason that God has not destroyed these modern day Sodoms is that Catholic nuns and priests live in these cities, and God does not wish to destroy them. He does, however, give these people body lice and hepatitis. It's so hard to know why God allows wickedness to flourish. I guess it's because God wants man to choose goodness freely of his own free will; sometimes one wonders if free will is worth all the trouble if there's going to be so much evil and unhappiness, but God knows best, presumably. If it were up to me, I might be tempted to wipe out cities and civilizations, but luckily for New York and Amsterdam, I'm not God. (*Reads.*) Why is St. Christopher no longer a saint, and did anyone listen to the prayers I prayed to him before they decided he didn't exist? The name Christopher means Christ-bearer and we used to believe that he carried the Christ child across a river on his shoulders. Then sometime around Pope John XXIII, the Catholic Church decided that this was just a story and didn't really happen. I am not convinced that when we get to heaven we may not find that St. Christopher *does* indeed exist and that he dislikes Pope John XXIII; however, if he does not exist, then the prayers you prayed to him would have been picked up by St. Jude. St. Jude is the patron saint of hopeless causes. When you have a particularly terrible problem that has little hope of being solved, you pray to St. Jude. When you lose or misplace something, you pray to St. Anthony. (*Reads.*) Tell us some more about your family. (*Smiles, pleased.*) I had 26 brothers and sisters. From my family 5 became priests, 7 became nuns, 3 became brothers, and the rest were institutionalized. My mother was also institutionalized shortly after she started thinking my father was

Satan. Some days when we were little, we'd come home
and not be able to find our mother so we'd pray to St. Anthony to help us find her. Then when we'd find her with her
head in the oven, we would pray to St. Jude to make her
sane again. Are all our prayers answered? Yes, they are;
what people who ask that question often don't realize is that
sometimes the answer to our prayer is "no." Dear God,
please make my mother not be crazy. God's answer: no.
Dear God, please let me recover from cancer. God's answer:
no. Dear God, please take away this toothache. God's answer: alright, but you're going to be run over by a car. But
every bad thing that happens to us, God has a special
reason for. God is the good shepherd, we are His flock. And
if God is grouchy or busy with more important matters, His
beloved mother Mary is always there to intercede for us. I
shall now sing the Hail Mary in Latin. (*Sister motions to
the lighting booth, and the lights change to an apparently
pre-arranged special spotlight for her, atmospheric with
blue spill and back lighting; the rest of the stage becomes
fairly dim. Sings.*)

> Ave Maria,
> Gratia plena,
> Maria, gratia plena,
> Maria, gratia plena,
> Ave, Ave! . . . (etc.)

(*As Sister sings, enter four people, ages 28–30. They are a
woman dressed as the Blessed Mother, a man dressed as St.
Joseph, and two people, a man and a woman, dressed as a
camel. The Blessed Mother sits on the back of the camel,
which is lead in by St. Joseph. Because of the dim lighting,
we don't see them too clearly at first. Sister, either sensing
something happening due to the audience or else just by
turning her head, suddenly sees them and is terribly startled
and confused.*)

ST. JOSEPH. We're sorry we're late.

SISTER. Oh dear God. (*Kneels.*)

ST. JOSEPH. Sister, what are you doing?

SISTER. You look so real.

ST. JOSEPH. Sister, I'm Gary Sullavan, and (*Pointing to the Blessed Mother.*) this is Diane Symonds. We were in your 5th grade class in 1959, and you asked us to come today. Don't you remember?

SISTER. 1959?

GARY. Don't you remember asking us?

SISTER. Not very distinctly. (*Louder, to lighting booth.*) Could I have some lights please? (*Lights come back up to where they were before. To Gary.*) What did I want you to do?

GARY. You wanted us to put on a pageant.

SISTER. That camel looks false to me.

PHILOMENA. Hello, Sister. (*She's the front of the camel.*)

SISTER. I thought so.

PHILOMENA. It's Philomena, Sister. Philomena Rostovitch.

ALOYSIUS. And Aloysius Benheim. (*He's the back of the camel.*)

SISTER. I don't really recognize any of you. Of course, you're not in your school uniforms.

DIANE. 1959.

SISTER. What?

DIANE. You taught us in 1959.

SISTER. I recognize you. Mary Jean Mahoney?

DIANE. I'm not Mary Jean Mahoney. I'm Diane Symonds.

SISTER. This is all so confusing.

GARY. Don't you want to see the pageant?

SISTER. What pageant is it?

GARY. We used to perform it at Christmas in your class; every class did. You said it was written in 1948 by Mary Jean Mahoney, who was your best student, you said.

DIANE. You said she was very elevated, and that when she was in the 7th grade she didn't have her first period, she had a stigmata.

SISTER. Oh yes. They discovered it in gym class. Mary Jean Mahoney. She entered a cloistered order of nuns upon her graduation from 12th grade. Sometimes late at night I can hear her praying. Mary Jean Mahoney. Yes, let's see her pageant again. (*To audience.*) She was such a bright student. (*Vague.*) I remember asking them to come now, I think. I wanted to tell you about Mary Jean Mahoney, and the perfect faith of a child. Yes, the pageant, please. Thomas, come watch with me. (*Thomas enters and sits on Sister's lap.*)

GARY. (*Announcing.*) The pageant of the birth and death of Our Beloved Saviour Jesus Christ, by Mary Jean Mahoney as told to Mrs. Robert J. Mahoney. The setting: a desert near Bethlehem. St. Joseph and the Virgin Mary and their trusty camel must flee from the wicked King Herod.

DIANE. (*Sings; to tune of "We Gather Together to ask the Lord's Blessings."*)

Hello, my name's Mary,
And his name is Joseph,
We're parents of Jesus,
Who's not been born yet,

We're fleeing from Herod,
And nobody knows if,
We'll make it to the town,
But we'll try, you can bet.

And I'm still a virgin,
And he's not the father,
The father descended
From heaven above,

And this is our camel,
He's really not much bother,
We're off to Bethlehem,
Because God is love.

GARY. Here's an Inn, Mary. But there doesn't look like there's any room.

DIANE. Well ask them, Joseph.

GARY. (*Knocks on imaginary door.*) Excuse me, you don't have room at this Inn, do you? (*Listens.*) He said they don't, Mary.

DIANE. Oh dear. Well let's try another Inn.

GARY. (*Knocks.*) Excuse me, you don't have room at this Inn, do you? (*Listens.*) He says they don't allow camels.

DIANE. Let's try the third Inn.

GARY. (*Knocks.*) Excuse me, you don't have room at your Inn, do you? (*Listens.*) I thought not . . . what? You would? Oh, Mary, this kind Innkeeper says that even though he has no room at the Inn, we can sleep in his stable.

DIANE. Do I look like a barn animal?

GARY. Mary, we really haven't any choice.

DIANE. Yes we do. Sister says we have choice over everything, because God gave us free will to decide between good and evil. And so I choose to stay in the stable.

GARY. Well here it is.

DIANE. Pew. It smells just like the zoo Mommy took me and Cynthia to visit last summer. We liked to look at the animals, but we didn't like to smell them.

GARY. I don't think there are any sheets.

DIANE. I don't need sheets, I'm so tired, I could sleep anywhere.

GARY. Well, that's good. Good night, Mary.

DIANE. But I do need pillows.

GARY. Mary, what can I do? We don't have any pillows.

DIANE. I can't sleep without pillows.

GARY. Let's pray to God then. If you just pray, he answers your prayers.

DIANE. Sometimes he says no, Joseph.

GARY. I know, but let's try. Dear God, we beseech thee, hear our prayer.

DIANE. Pillows! Pillows! Pillows!

GARY. And behold God answered their prayers.

CAMEL. (*Philomena.*) We have an idea, Mary and Joseph. We have two humps, and you can use them as pillows.

DIANE. Thank you, God! Come on, Joseph. Let's go to sleep.

CAMEL. (*As Mary and Joseph start to sleep, sings a lullaby:*)

> Rockabye, and good night,
> May God keep you and watch you,
> Rockabye, and good night, (etc.)

(*They sleep. Aloysius makes baby crying noises, tosses out a doll onto the floor.*)

DIANE. (*Seeing the doll.*) Joseph, He's born. Jesus is born.

GARY, DIANE, and CAMEL. (*Sing.*)

> Joy to the world, the Saviour's come,
> Let earth receive her king,
> La la la la la la la la,
> La la la la la la la la,
> Let heaven and nature sing,
> Let heaven and nature sing,
> Let heaven, and heaven, and nature sing!

GARY. (*To doll.*) Can you say Poppa, Jesus? Can you say Momma?

DIANE. He's not that kind of child, Joseph. He was born without original sin like me. This is called my Immaculate Conception, which is not to be confused with my Virgin Birth. Everyone makes this error, it makes me lose my patience. *We* must learn from *him,* Joseph.

GARY. (*To audience.*) And so Jesus instructed His parents, and the priests in the Temple, and He said many unusual things, many of them irritating to parents. Things like "Before Abraham was, I am." And "Do you not know that I must go about my father's business?" after we'd been worried to death and unable to find Him after looking for hours and hours. And He performed many miracles.

DIANE. He turned water into wine.

GARY. He made cripples walk.

DIANE. He walked on the water.

GARY. And then came the time for His crucifixion. And His mother said to him:

DIANE. (*To doll.*) But why, Jesus, why? Why must you be crucified? And what do you mean by "I must die so that others may know eternal life"?

GARY. And Jesus explained that because Adam and Eve, especially Eve, had sinned that mankind was cursed until Jesus could redeem us by dying on the cross.

DIANE. But that sounds silly. Why can't God just forgive us? And it's Adam and Eve anyway, not us.

GARY. But Jesus laughed at her and He said, "Yours is not to reason why, yours is but to do and die." And then He said, "But seriously, mother, it is not up to God to justify His ways to man; rather man must have total and complete faith in God's wisdom, he must accept and not question, just like an innocent babe accepts and doesn't question his mommy and daddy." And then Mary said:

DIANE. I understand. Or rather, I understand that I am not supposed to understand. Come, let us go to Golgotha and watch you be crucified.

GARY. And Mary and the apostles and the faithful camel, whose name was Misty, followed Jesus to the rock of Golgotha and watched Him be nailed to a cross. (*Gary has a hammer and nails, and nails the doll to a little cross; then stands it up that way.*)

DIANE. And Jesus looked at the two thieves crucified on either side of Him, and He said to one:

GARY. Thou art saved; and to the other, He said:

DIANE. Thou art condemned for all eternity.

GARY. And then He hung there for three hours in terrible agony.

DIANE. Imagine the agony. Try to feel the nails ripping through His hands and feet. Pound, pound, pound, rip, rip, rip. Washing the dishes for three hours is nothing compared to hanging on a cross.

GARY. And then He died. He's dead now, Mary.

DIANE. (*Sad, lost.*) Oh.

GARY. Let's go for a long walk.

DIANE. Oh, Joseph, I feel so alone.

GARY. So do I, Mary.

DIANE. (*Truly wondering.*) Do you think He was just a nut? Do you think maybe the Holy Ghost isn't His Father at all, that I made it all up? Maybe I'm not a virgin . . . Maybe . . .

GARY. But then Misty said . . .

CAMEL. (*Philomena.*) Do not despair, Mary and Joseph. Of course, He is God, He'll rise again in three days.

DIANE. If only I could believe you. But why should I listen to a dumb animal?

CAMEL. (*Philomena.*) O ye, of little faith.

DIANE. (*Sad.*) Oh, Joseph, I'm losing my mind.

SISTER: *Thomas, come read this partial list of those who are going to burn in hell.*
THOMAS: *Christine Keeler, Roman Polanski, Zsa Zsa Gabor, the editors of* After Dark *magazine, Linda Lovelace, Georgina Spelvin, Big John Holmes, Brooke Shields, David Bowie, Mick Jagger, Patty Hearst, Betty Comden, Adolph Green.*
SISTER: *This is just a partial list. It is added to constantly.*

GARY:...and then Jesus came out from behind the tree where He was hiding, they spent forty days on earth enjoying themselves and setting the groundwork for the Catholic Church, and then Jesus, Mary, Joseph and Misty ascended into heaven and lived happily ever after.

GEORGE: *Are we, on a guess, waiting for Godot?*
ELLEN TERRY: *No, Willie. He came. already and was an awful bore.*

*VOICE: Ladies and gentlemen, may I have your attention please?
At this evening's performance, the role of Sir Thomas More, the
man for all seasons, normally played by Edwin Booth, will be
played by George Spelvin....And at this evening's performance
the executioner will play himself.*
*GEORGE: What does he mean, the executioner will play himself?
...Oh, sir, there's been an error. I think it's fine if the King marries
Anne Boleyn....*

photographs © 1981 Susan Cook

GARY. And so Mary and Joseph and the camel hid for three days and three nights, and on Sunday morning they got up and went to the Tomb where Christ was buried. And when they got there, standing by the Tomb was an angel. And the angel spoke.

ALOYSIUS. (*Back of camel.*) Mary and Joseph, your son has risen from the dead, just like your dumb animal Misty told you He would.

DIANE. I can't see the angel, can you, Joseph?

ALOYSIUS. O doubting Thomases of the world, must you see and touch everything in order to believe? Mary and Joseph! Your son Jesus wishes you to go out into the world and tell the people that unless they have the faith of the dumb animal Misty they shall not enter the Kingdom of Heaven. For, yea I say to you, at the end of the world the first in the class will be the last in the class, the boy with A in arithmetic will get F, the girl with F in geography will get A, and those with brains will be cast down in favor of those who are like dumb animals. For thus are the ways of the Lord.

GARY. And then Mary and Joseph, realizing their lack of faith, thanked Misty and made a good Act of Contrition. And then Jesus came out from behind the tree where He was hiding, they spent forty days on earth enjoying themselves and setting the groundwork for the Catholic Church, and then Jesus, Mary, Joseph and Misty ascended into heaven and lived happily ever after. (*Diane and Gary, holding the doll between them, stand in front of the camel. All sing the final jubilant phrase of "Angels We Have Heard on High" Christmas carol, as Diane and Gary mime ascension by waving their arms in a flying motion.*)

ALL. (*Singing.*)

Glor-or-or-or-ia! In Excelsis Deo!

(*All four bow. Sister applauds enthusiastically. After their bow, the four quickly get out of their costumes, continuing*

*to do so during some of Sister's next speech if necessary.
Their "regular" clothes are indeed regular and not too
noteworthy: Diane might wear slacks or jeans but with an
attractive sweater or blouse and with a blazer, Gary might
wear chinos, a nice shirt with even a tie, or a vest—casual
but neat, pleasant; Philomena might wear a dress, Aloysius
a shirt and slacks [or, if played as a bit formal, even a
suit].)*

SISTER. Oh, thank you, children. That was lovely. Thank
you. (*To audience.*) The old stories really are the best,
aren't they? Mary Jean Mahoney. What a good child. And
what a nice reunion *we're* having. What year did you say
you were in my class again?

GARY. 1959.

SISTER. 1959. Oh, those were happy years. Eisenhower,
Pope Pius still alive, then the first Catholic president. And
so now you've all grown up. Let's do some of the old questions, shall we? (*To Aloysius.*) Who made you?

ALOYSIUS. God made me.

SISTER. Quite correct. What is the seventh commandment?

PHILOMENA. The seventh commandment is thou shalt not
steal.

SISTER. Very good. (*To Diane.*) What is contrition? You.

DIANE. Uh . . . being sorry for sin?

SISTER. (*Cheerfully chastising.*) That's not how we answer
questions here, young lady. Thomas?

THOMAS. Contrition is sincere sorrow for having offended
God, and hatred for the sins we have committed, with a
firm purpose of sinning no more.

DIANE. Oh yes. Right.

SISTER. (*Still kindly.*) For someone who's just played the
Virgin, you don't know your catechism responses very well.
What grade are you in?

DIANE. I'm not in a grade. I'm in life.

SISTER. Oh yes, right. Well, cookies anyone? Thomas, go bring our nice guests some cookies. (*Thomas exits.*) It's so nice to see you all again. You must all be married by now, I imagine. I hope you all have large families like we encouraged?

PHILOMENA. I have a little girl, age three.

SISTER. That's nice.

ALOYSIUS. I have two boys.

SISTER. I like boys. (*To Gary.*) And you?

GARY. I'm not married.

SISTER. Well, a nice looking boy like you, it won't be long before some pretty girl snatches you up. (*To Diane.*) And you?

DIANE. I don't have any children. But I've had two abortions.

(*Sister is stunned. Enter Thomas with cookies.*)

SISTER. No cookies, Thomas. Take them away. (*Thomas exits immediately. To Diane.*) You are in a state of mortal sin, young woman. What is the fifth commandment?

DIANE. Thou shalt not kill.

SISTER. You are a murderer.

DIANE. (*Unemotional.*) The first one was when I was raped when I was eighteen.

SISTER. Well I am sorry to hear that. But only God has power over life and death. God might have had very special plans for your baby. Are you sure I taught you?

DIANE. Yes you taught me.

SISTER. Did I give you good grades?

DIANE. Yes. Very good.

SISTER. Have you told these sins in confession?

DIANE. What sins?

SISTER. You know very well what I mean.

DIANE. I don't go to confession.

SISTER. Well, it looks pretty clear to me, we'll just add you to the list of people going to hell. (*Calling.*) Thomas, we'll put her name right after Comden and Green. Somebody, change the subject. I don't want to hear any more about this.

GARY. (*Trying to oblige.*) Ummmm . . . it certainly is strange being able to chew the communion wafer now, isn't it?

SISTER. What?

GARY. Well, you used to tell us that because the communion wafer was really the body of Christ, if we chewed it, it might bleed.

SISTER. I was speaking metaphorically.

GARY. Oh.

SISTER. (*Pause.*) Well, I still feel shaken by that girl over there. (*Points to Diane.*) Let's talk about something positive. You, with the little girl. Tell me about yourself.

PHILOMENA. Well my little girl is three, and her name is Wendy.

SISTER. There is no Saint Wendy.

PHILOMENA. Her middle name is Mary.

SISTER. Wendy Mary. Too many y's. I'd change it. What does your husband do?

PHILOMENA. I don't have a husband. (*Long pause.*)

SISTER. Did he die?

PHILOMENA. I don't think so. I didn't know him for very long.

SISTER. Do you sign your letters Mrs. or Miss?

PHILOMENA. I don't write letters.

SISTER. Did this person you lost track of *marry* you before he left?

PHILOMENA. (*Sad.*) No.

SISTER. Children, you are making me very sad. (*To Philomena.*) Did you get good grades in my class?

PHILOMENA. No, Sister. You said I was stupid.

SISTER. Are you a prostitute?

PHILOMENA. Sister! Certainly not. I just get lonely.

SISTER. The Mother Superior of my own convent may get lonely, but does she have illegitimate children?

ALOYSIUS. There was that nun who stuffed her baby behind her dresser last year. (*Sister stares at him.*) It was in the news.

SISTER. No one was addressing you, Aloysius. Philomena, my point is that loneliness does not excuse sin.

PHILOMENA. But there are worse sins. And I believe Jesus forgives me. After all, he didn't want them to stone the woman taken in adultery.

SISTER. That was merely a *political* gesture. In private Christ stoned *many* women taken in adultery.

DIANE. That's not in the Bible.

SISTER. (*Suddenly very angry.*) Not everything has to be in the Bible! (*To audience, trying to recoup.*) There's oral tradition within the Church. One priest tells another priest something, it gets passed down through the years.

PHILOMENA. (*Unhappy.*) But don't you believe Jesus forgives people who sin?

SISTER. Yes, of course, He forgives sin, but He's *tricky*. You have to be *truly* sorry, and you have to *truly* resolve not to sin again, or else He'll send you straight to hell just like the thief He was crucified next to.

PHILOMENA. I think Jesus forgives me.

SISTER. Well I think you're going to hell. (*To Aloysius.*) And what about you? Is there anything the matter with you?

ALOYSIUS. Nothing. I'm fine.

SISTER. But are you living properly?

ALOYSIUS. Yes.

SISTER. And you're married?

ALOYSIUS. Yes.

SISTER. And you don't use birth control?

ALOYSIUS. No.

SISTER. But you only have two children. Why is that? You're not spilling your seed like Onan, are you? That's a sin, you know.

ALOYSIUS. No. It's just chance that we haven't had more.

SISTER. And you go to Mass once a week, and communion at least once a year, and confession at least once a year? Right?

ALOYSIUS. Yes.

SISTER. Well I'm very pleased then.

ALOYSIUS. I am an alcoholic, and recently I've started to hit my wife, and I keep thinking about suicide.

SISTER. Within bounds, all those things are venial sins. At least one of my students turned out well. Of course, I don't know how hard you're hitting your wife; but with prayer and God's grace . . .

ALOYSIUS. My wife is very unhappy.

SISTER. Yes, but eventually there's death. And then everlasting happiness in heaven. Some days I long for heaven. (*To Gary.*) And you? Have you turned out all right?

GARY. I'm okay.

SISTER. And you don't use birth control?

GARY. Definitely not.

SISTER. That's good. (*Looks at him.*) What do you mean, "definitely not"?

GARY. I don't use it.

SISTER. And you're not married. Have you not found the right girl?

GARY. (*Evasively.*) In a manner of speaking.

SISTER. (*Grim.*) Okay. You do that thing that makes Jesus puke, don't you?

GARY. Pardon?

SISTER. Drop the polite boy manners, buster. When your mother looks at you, she turns into a pillar of salt, right?

GARY. What?

SISTER. Sodom and Gomorrha, stupid. You sleep with men, don't you?

GARY. Well . . . yes.

SISTER. Jesus, Mary, and Joseph! We have a regular cross section in here.

GARY. I got seduced when I was in the seminary. I mean, I guess I'd been denying it up to then.

SISTER. We don't want to hear about it.

GARY. And then when I left the seminary I was very upset, and then I went to New York and I slept with five hundred different people.

SISTER. Jesus is going to throw up.

GARY. But then I decided I was trashing my life, and so I only had sex with guys I had an emotional relationship with.

SISTER. That must have cut it down to about 300.

GARY. And now I'm living with this one guy who I'd gone to grade school with and only ran into again two years ago, and we're faithful with one another and stuff. He was in your class too. Jeff Hannigan.

SISTER. He was a bad boy. Some of them should be left on the side of a hill to die, and he was one.

GARY. You remember him?

SISTER. Not really. His type.

GARY. Anyway, when I met him again, he was still a practicing Catholic, and so now I am again too.

SISTER. I'd practice a little harder if I were you.

GARY. So I don't think I'm so bad.

SISTER. (*Vomit sound.*) Blah. You make me want to blah. Didn't any of you listen to me when I was teaching you? What were you all doing? (*Mad, trying to set the record straight again.*) There is the universe, created by God. Eve ate the apple, man got original sin, God sent down Jesus to redeem us. Jesus said to St. Peter, "Upon this rock," rock meaning Peter, "I build my Church," by which he meant that Peter was the first Pope and that he and the subsequent Popes would be infallible on matters of doctrine and morals. So your way is very clear: you have this infallible Church that tells you what is right and wrong, and you follow its teaching, and then you get to heaven. Didn't you all *hear* me say that? Did you all have wax in your ears? Did I speak in a foreign lanuage? Or what? And you've all sinned against sex— (*To Aloysius.*) not you, you're just depressed, you probably need vitamins—but the rest of you. Why this obsession with sex? The Church has been very clear setting up the guidelines for you. (*To Philomena and Diane.*) For you two girls, why can't you simply marry one Catholic man and have as many babies as chance and the good Lord allows you to? Simple, easy to follow directions. (*To Gary.*) And for you, you can *force* yourself to marry and procreate with some nice Catholic girl—try it, it's not so hard—or you can be celibate for the rest of your life. Again, simple advice. (*Suddenly furious.*) Those are your options! No others. They are your direct paths to heaven and salvation, to everlasting happiness! Why aren't you following these paths? Are you insane?

DIANE. You're insane.

SISTER. You know, you're my least favorite person here today. I mean, the little effeminate one over there (*Points to Gary.*) makes me want to blah, but I can tell he once was nice, and he might get better with shock treatments and aversion therapy. But I can tell shock treatments wouldn't help you. You're fresh as paint, and you're nasty. I can see it in your face.

DIANE. You shouldn't be teaching children. You should be locked up in a convent where you can't hurt anybody.

SISTER. Me hurt someone. You're the one who runs around killing babies at the drop of a hat.

DIANE. It's a medical procedure. And even the Church admits it can't pinpoint *when* life begins in the womb. Why should you decide that the minute the sperm touches the ovum that . . .

SISTER. Don't talk filth to me, I don't want to hear it. (*Suddenly very suspicious.*) Why did you all come here today? I don't remember asking you.

GARY. It was Diane's idea.

SISTER. What? What was?

PHILOMENA. We wanted to embarrass you.

ALOYSIUS. None of us ever liked you.

SISTER. What do you mean? My students always loved me. I was the favorite.

ALOYSIUS. No. We thought you were a bully.

SISTER. I was the *favorite*.

ALOYSIUS. You never let me go to the bathroom when I needed to.

SISTER. All you had to do was raise your hand.

ALOYSIUS. There were sixty children, and I sat in the back of the room; and I did raise my hand, but you never acknowledged me. Every afternoon my bladder became very full, and I always ended up wetting my pants.

SISTER. Big deal.

ALOYSIUS. I spoke to you about recognizing me sooner, and about my problem, but all you said then was "big deal."

SISTER. I remember you. You used to make a puddle in the last row every day.

ALOYSIUS. I have bladder problems to this day.

SISTER. What a baby. You flunked. I was giving you a lesson in life, and you flunked. It was up to you to solve the problem: don't drink your little carton of milk at lunch; bring a little container with you and urinate behind your desk; or simply hold it in and offer the discomfort up to Christ. He suffered three hours of agony on the cross, surely a full bladder pales by comparison. I talk about the universe and original sin and heaven and hell, and you complain to me about bathroom privileges. You're a ridiculous crybaby. (*Cuffs him on the head.*)

PHILOMENA. You used to hit me too.

SISTER. You probably said stupid things.

PHILOMENA. I did. I told you I was stupid. That was no reason to hit me.

SISTER. It seems a very good reason to hit you. Knock some sense into you.

PHILOMENA. You used to take the point of your pencil and poke it up and down on my head when I didn't do my homework.

SISTER. You should have done your homework.

PHILOMENA. And when I didn't know how to do long division, you slammed my head against the blackboard.

SISTER. Did I ever break a bone?

PHILOMENA. No.

SISTER. There, you see! (*To Gary.*) And what about you?

GARY. You didn't do anything to me in particular. I just found you scary.

SISTER. Well I am scary.

GARY. But my lover Jeff doesn't like you cause you made him wet his pants too.

SISTER. All this obsession with the bladder. (*To Diane.*) And you, the nasty one, why did you want to embarrass me?

DIANE. (*Said simply.*) Because I believed you. I believed how you said the world worked, and that God loved us, and the story of the Good Shepherd and the lost sheep; and I don't think you should lie to people.

SISTER. But that's how things are. I didn't lie.

DIANE. When I was sixteen, my mother got breast cancer, which spread. I prayed to God to let her suffering be small, but her suffering seemed to me quite extreme. She was in bad pain for half a year, and then terrible pain for much of a full year. The ulcerations on her body were horrifying to her and to me. Her last few weeks she slipped into a semiconscious state, which allowed her, unfortunately, to wake up for a few minutes at a time and to have a full awareness of her pain and her fear of death. She was able to recognize me, and she would try to cry, but she was unable to; and to speak, but she was unable to. I think she wanted me to get

her new doctors; she never really accepted that her disease
was going to kill her, and she thought in her panic that her
doctors must be incompetent and that new ones could magi-
cally cure her. Then, thank goodness, she went into a full
coma. A nurse who I knew to be Catholic assured me that
everything would be done to keep her alive—a dubious com-
fort. Happily, the doctor was not Catholic, or if he was, not
doctrinaire, and they didn't use extraordinary means to keep
her alive; and she finally died after several more weeks in
her coma. Now there are, I'm sure, far worse deaths—terrible burnings, tortures, plague, pestilence, famine; Christ on
the cross even, as Sister likes to say. But I thought my
mother's death was bad enough, and I got confused as to
why I had been praying and to whom. I mean, if prayer was
really this sort of button you pressed—admit you need the
Lord, then He stops your suffering—then why didn't it always work? Or ever work? And when it worked, so-called,
and our prayers were supposedly answered, wasn't it as
likely to be chance as God? God always answers our
prayers, you said, He just sometimes says no. But why
would He say no to stopping my mother's suffering? I
wasn't even asking that she live, just that He end her suffering. And it can't be that He was letting her suffer because
she'd been bad, because she hadn't been bad and besides
suffering doesn't seem to work that way, considering the
suffering of children who've obviously done nothing wrong.
So why was He letting her suffer? Spite? Was the Lord
God actually malicious? That seemed possible, but far
fetched. Maybe He had no control over it, maybe He wasn't
omnipotent as you taught us He was. Maybe He created the
world sort of by accident by belching one morning or get-
ting the hiccups, and maybe He had no idea how the whole
thing worked. In which case, He wouldn't be malicious, just
useless. Or, of course, more likely than that, He didn't exist
at all, the universe was hiccupped or belched into existence
all on its own, and my mother's suffering just existed like
rain or wind or humidity. I became angry at myself, and by
extension at you, for ever having expected anything beyond
randomness from the world. And while I was thinking these

things, the day that my mother died, I was raped. Now I know that's really too much, one really loses all sympathy for me because I sound like I'm making it up or something. But bad things sometimes happen all at once, and this particular day on my return from the hospital I was raped by some maniac who broke into the house. He had a knife and cut me up some. Anyway, I don't really want to go on about the experience, but I got very depressed for about 5 years. Somehow the utter randomness of things—my mother's suffering, my attack by a lunatic who was either born a lunatic or made one by cruel parents or perhaps by an imbalance of hormones or whatever, etc. etc.—*this randomness seemed intolerable.* I found I grew to hate you, Sister, for making me once expect everything to be ordered and to make sense. My psychiatrist said he thought my hatred of you was obsessive, that I just was looking for someone to blame. Then he seduced me, and he was the father of my second abortion.

SISTER. I think she's making all this up.

DIANE. He said I seduced him. And maybe that's so. But he could be lying just to make himself feel better. (*To Sister.*) And of course your idea that I should have had this baby, either baby, is preposterous. Have you any idea what a terrible mother I'd be? I'm a nervous wreck.

SISTER. God would have given you the strength.

DIANE. I suppose it is childish to look for blame, part of the randomness of things is that there is no one to blame; but basically I think everything is your fault, Sister.

SISTER. You have obviously never read the Book of Job.

DIANE. I have read it. And I think it's a nasty story.

SISTER. God explains in that story why He lets us suffer, and a very lovely explanation it is too. He likes to test us so that when we choose to love Him no matter what He does to us that proves how great and deep our love for Him is.

DIANE. That sounds like "The Story of O."

SISTER. Well there's obviously no talking to you. You don't want help or knowledge or enlightenment, so there's nothing left for you but an unhappy life, sickness, death, and hell.

DIANE. Last evening I killed my psychiatrist and now I'm going to kill you. (*Takes out a gun.*)

GARY. Oh dear. I thought we were just going to embarrass her.

SISTER. (*Stalling for time.*) And you have, very much so. So no need to kill me at all. Goodbye, Diane, Gary, Aloysius . . .

DIANE. You're insane. You shouldn't be allowed to teach children. I see that there's that little boy here today. You're going to make him crazy.

SISTER. Thomas, stay off-stage with the cookies, dear.

DIANE. I want you to admit that everything's your fault, and then I'm going to kill you.

PHILOMENA. Maybe we should all wait outside.

SISTER. Stay here. Diane, look at me. I was wrong. I admit it. I'm sorry. I thought everything made sense, but I didn't understand things properly. There's nothing I can say to make it up to you but. . . . (*Seeing something awful behind Diane's head.*) LOOK OUT! (*Diane looks behind her, Sister whips out her own gun and shoots Diane dead. Sister like a circus artist completing a stunt, hands up:*) Ta-da! For those non-Catholics present, murder is allowable in self-defense, one doesn't even have to tell it in confession. Thomas, bring me some water.

GARY. We didn't know she was bringing a gun. (*Thomas brings water.*)

SISTER. I remember her now from class. (*Looks at her dead body.*) She had no sense of humor.

ALOYSIUS. I have to go to the bathroom.

SISTER. (*Aims gun at him.*) Stay where you are. Raise your hand if you want to go to the bathroom, Aloysius, and wait until I have acknowledged you. (*She ignores him now, though keeps gun aimed at him most of the time.*) Thomas, bring me a cookie. (*He does.*) Most of my students turned out beautifully, these are the few exceptions. But we never give up on those who've turned out badly, do we, Thomas? What is the story of the Good Shepherd and the Lost Sheep?

THOMAS. The Good Shepherd was so concerned about his Lost Sheep that he left his flock to go find the Lost Sheep, and then He found it.

SISTER. That's right. And while he was gone, a great big wolf came and killed his entire flock. No, just kidding, I'm feeling lightheaded from all this excitement. No, by the story of the Lost Sheep, Christ tells us that when a sinner strays we mustn't give up on the sinner. (*Sister indicates for Thomas to exit, he does.*) So I don't totally despair for these people standing here. Gary, I hope that you will leave your friend Jeff, don't even tell him where you're going, just disappear, and then I hope you will live your life as a celibate. Like me. Celibate rhymes with celebrate. Our Lord loves celibate people. And you, Philomena, I hope you will get married to some nice Catholic man, or if you stay unmarried then you too will become a celibate. Rhymes with celebrate.

ALOYSIUS. Sister, I have my hand up.

SISTER. Keep it up. And you, Aloysius, I hope you'll remember not to kill yourself, which is a mortal sin. For if we live by God's laws even though we are having a miserable life, remember heaven and eternal happiness are our reward.

GARY. Should we help you with the body, Sister?

SISTER. The janitor will help me later, thank you. You two may go now, so I can finish my lecture.

GARY. Why don't you let him go to the bathroom?

SISTER. Gary?

GARY. Yes, Sister?

SISTER. You still believe what you do with Jeff is wrong, don't you? I mean, you still confess it in confession, don't you?

GARY. Well I don't really think it's wrong, but I'm not sure, so I do still tell it in confession.

SISTER. When did you last go to confession?

GARY. This morning actually. I was going to be playing Saint Joseph and all.

SISTER. And you haven't sinned since then, have you?

GARY. No, Sister. (*Sister shoots him dead.*)

SISTER. (*Triumphantly.*) I've sent him to heaven! (*To Philomena.*) Okay, you with the little girl, go home before I decide your little girl would be better off in a Catholic orphanage. (*Philomena exits in terror. To audience.*) I'm not really within the letter of the law shooting Gary like this, but really if he did make a good confession I have sent him straight to heaven and eternal, blissful happiness. And I'm afraid otherwise he would have ended up in hell. I think Christ will allow me this little dispensation from the letter of the law, but I'll go to confession later today, just to be sure.

ALOYSIUS. Sister, I have to go to the bathroom.

SISTER. Wait until I recognize you, Aloysius.

ALOYSIUS. I'm going to leave now.

SISTER. (*Angry, emphasizing the gun.*) I've used this twice today, don't tempt me to use it again. Thomas! (*He enters.*) Who made you?

THOMAS. God made me.

SISTER. Why did God make you?

THOMAS. God made me to show forth his goodness and to share with us His happiness.

ALOYSIUS. If you don't let me go to the bathroom, I'm going to wet my pants.

SISTER. We all have free will, Aloysius. Thomas, explain about the primary cause again.

THOMAS. Everything has a primary cause. Dinner is put on the table because the primary cause . . .

SISTER. Thomas, I'm going to nap some, I'm exhausted. (*Hands him gun.*) You keep that dangerous man over there covered, and if he moves shoot him; and also recite some nice catechism questions for us all while I rest. All right, dear?

THOMAS. Yes, Sister. (*Sister sits on a chair and naps. Thomas sits on her lap, aiming the gun at Aloysius, and recites from memory.*)
     "What must we do to gain the happiness of heaven?"
     To gain the happiness of heaven, we must know, love, and serve God in this world.
     (*Lights start to dim.*)
     "From whom do we learn to know, love and serve God?"
     We learn to know, love, and serve God from Jesus Christ, the Son of God, who teaches us through the Catholic Church.
     "What are some of the perfections of God?"
     Some of the perfections of God are: God is eternal, all-good, all-knowing, all-present, and almighty.
     (*Lights have dimmed to black.*)

ADDENDUM (*Author's Notes*)

Since scripts are so open to interpretations, I wanted to suggest some things to avoid, as well as to aim for, in presenting this play; and to make a few clarifications.

The casting of Sister Mary is obviously of the utmost importance. In casting for the Ensemble Studio Theatre production, we saw a great many different types for Sister; and these auditions were helpful in suggesting the various pitfalls of casting and playing the role.

For starters, it's a mistake to have an actress play (or, worse, seem to be) mean. Though a strident, bullying approach may work in an audition and even be funny, it can't really sustain for the whole play; we see Sister kill two people at the end of the play, we shouldn't expect her to do so five minutes after we first see her. (There are places, of course, where Sister *should* be strident and bullying; but it should be underneath and revealed only sometimes.) Also, perhaps more importantly, the strength and power of figures like Sister Mary (or, say, Jean Brodie) is in their charm; we believe them because they take us in. If Sister were obviously a horror, we'd know not to believe her.

In line with this, the relationship between Sister and Thomas should have warmth and even love. It's true that she presents him as one might present a dog doing tricks; and yet he does all the tricks well, and she rewards him with not only cookies but warmth, approval, bounces on the knee, etc. All this fondness and attention could easily make Thomas adore Sister.

The actress playing Sister should avoid commenting on her role. (All the actors should avoid commenting.) The humor works best when presented straight. That is, it's fine that we as an audience think it outrageous that Sister contemplates Thomas' castration to save his pretty voice; the actress should not indicate her own awareness of this outrageousness (that kind of comic-wink acting that is effective sometimes in a skit, rarely in a play). Sister thinks nothing is wrong with her contemplation, and it's only her feelings we should see.

In terms of age range for Sister, anywhere between forty and sixty seems correct to me. The over-sixty, more grand-motherly-looking actresses we auditioned seemed to throw the play out of whack: they seemed less powerful and more dotty, and also we felt bad for them when the ex-students berated them.

It is possible to consider casting someone younger as Sister, though you will lose the important theatrical fact of having three generations on stage. However, depending on your casting resources, a younger Sister Mary with comic flair and believability is, of course, preferable to an older one with neither attribute.

One other thought in terms of casting: the excellent Sister Mary at E.S.T., Elizabeth Franz, also brought to the role a delicate femininity that was true to a certain kind of real-life nun, very much added to her charm with Thomas and with the audience, and was an extremely effective starting point that nowhere tipped off Sister's potential for murderous rages.

Thomas should be seven or eight, and be smart and polite. There should be no attempt to play up his being child (like having him not be able to read the list of names going to hell; he should read them easily). An older child could play it, but seven or eight has a genuine innocence that can't be faked—an innocence which is central to the play's meaning.

The tone of the pageant is tricky. It should be childlike, as opposed to childish. It is thirty year olds performing it, so they shouldn't pretend to be children, but they can't act like adults precisely either. They should be simple and direct, presenting the story as if we didn't know it and as if it didn't have a child's imprint on the writing. Lots of busy stage business making fun of clunky amateur productions will get in the way.

There is an enormous trap to be avoided in the playing of the four ex-students, and that centers around their apparent plot to come to Sister's lecture to "embarrass" her.

For starters, you mustn't play the plot as a subtext in the pageant or really anywhere before it's mentioned because the audience simply won't know what you're doing. Plus, there's a further trap: if you choose to play that the four have come to embarrass Sister by telling her how much they've strayed from her teaching (Philomena's illegitimate child, Gary's being gay), those revelation scenes won't work comically (as they're intended) because the comedy is based partially on Gary and Philomena not meaning to reveal what Sister drags out of them.

I think to make sense of the "plot" (happily, this is something the audience doesn't really have time to brood about) one would have to imagine Diane calling up the other three with an extremely *vague* plan: let's put on that old pageant, which is so silly and which will disrupt her lecture; then the "point" of the intrusion will be to eventually tell Sister that she's not fondly remembered (her temper, her not letting people go to the bathroom, etc.). Or maybe the plan is only to put on the pageant, just as a joke to themselves on their past. The vaguer you allow the plan to be in your head, the less saddled with unnecessary subtext you'll be and the more easily (and humorously) the various confrontations with Sister will play. (Diane's sense of the plan has to be different and darker than the others, of course, because she's packing a gun; but even she can be unsure of what she's going to do. Note: I do see the logic of Diane showing some of her bitterness and edge in the pageant, but I warn against it as confusing to the audience and as destructive to the enjoyment of the pageant.)

A final danger in playing the foursome: avoid kvetching (admittedly tricky since complaining *is* more or less what they're doing in some sections). With Philomena's complaints about being hit and with Aloysius' complaints about the bathroom, it's important to find a balance between the legitimate complaints (Sister was indeed spiteful) and the fact that Philomena and Aloysius are near thirty and that these things are in the past. Apropos of this, real horror and sense memory of what it was like not to go to the bathroom are to be avoided; if the complaints are presented too hysterically, the people will seem stupid and I don't want them to be stupid. It's difficult: I don't want them to be blase either. It's a balance that's needed, that sense of having the character know it's childish to still be angry but to nonetheless still be angry.

A word or two about Diane's monologue. It is obviously meant very seriously, but though it has a high emotional content, the actress should be very careful in how much emotion she lets through and when. In auditions, some actresses ranted and raved and wept in the speech, and it was ungodly. Diane's speech is very verbal, and very methodically point-by-point; hysteria is an illogical interpretation of the tone and content of what she's saying.

The speech has so much charged material (the mother's death, the rape) that one must also be careful not to *ask* for sympathy.

It might be helpful in approaching the speech to remember that what she describes happened many years ago (not that she's not traumatized, it's just that time has taken some of the immediacy away at least); and also that Diane tries to *distance* herself from the pain she feels by being analytic. The tone of much of the speech, whatever underlying sadness might come through, should be factual, her attempt at distancing herself: this happened to me, and then I thought that, but that wasn't true, so then I thought this and this, etc.

There is, though, probably a natural place (among other possibilities) for the anger and pain to break through all this distancing, and that's on "—this randomness seemed intolerable," which both follows a particularly futile attempt at reasoning things out (her run-on, off-the-point comments on what made the rapist a rapist) and is also the core of what she hates Sister for: making her expect and desire order where there doesn't seem to be any.

Some miscellaneous things:

At E.S.T. we cast Aloysius as an Italian street kid grown up, and changed his last name to Busiccio. This seemed to work fine, and is an option. The other option, I'd presume, is to present him as tense, formal, uptight, and of undetermined ancestry. (Note: with the latter option, be careful that the interpretation does not imply homosexuality in any way, which would throw the play's balance off.)

Gary is not meant to be effeminate. Sister's comment to that effect is meant to show her prejudice, not reflect any reality.

When Gary says "Definitely not" to Sister's query as to whether he uses birth control, I don't mean for him to be playing cat-and-mouse with her or to be making some smirking allusion to being gay; it's simply that he indeed doesn't use birth control and he says "definitely not" quickly, without thinking what it might imply. The scene plays comically if she draws these facts out of him unwittingly; otherwise we're back in the "revenge plot" trap again.

"Celibate" does not rhyme with "celebrate," nor (in my mind) does Sister think it does. I prefer that she pronounce both words properly and then says they rhyme because she wants them to; it sort of extends her power to say blatantly false things when she feels like it, to make a point (as when she says Christ stoned many women taken in adultery).

In production, we found having Sister's gun right in the lectern (out of sight) worked best, with Sister standing conveniently behind it. Having it in her habit seemed unworkable. Diane's gun, though, seemed to fit inside her blazer successfully.

THE
ACTOR'S
NIGHTMARE

THE ACTOR'S NIGHTMARE was first presented off-Broadway by Playwright's Horizons in New York City on October 14, 1981. It was directed by Jerry Zaks, with set design by Karen Schulz, costumes by William Ivey Long, lighting by Paul Gallo, and sound by Aural Fixation. The cast, in order of appearance, was as follows:

GEORGE SPELVIN	*Jeff Brooks*
MEG	*Polly Draper*
SARAH SIDDONS	*Elizabeth Franz*
DAME ELLEN TERRY	*Mary Catherine Wright*
HENRY IRVING	*Timothy Landfield*

Characters

GEORGE SPELVIN
MEG, the stage manager
SARAH SIDDONS
DAME ELLEN TERRY
HENRY IRVING

SCENE—*basically an empty stage, maybe with a few set pieces on it or around it.*
George Spelvin, a young man (20 to 30), wanders in. He looks baffled and uncertain about where he is.
Enter Meg, the stage manager. In jeans and sweat shirt, perhaps, pleasant, efficient, age 25 to 30 probably.

GEORGE: Oh, I'm sorry. I don't know how I got in here.

MEG: Oh thank goodness you're here. I've been calling you.

GEORGE: Pardon?

MEG: An awful thing has happened. Eddie's been in a car accident, and you'll have to go on for him.

GEORGE: Good heavens, how awful. Who's Eddie?

MEG: Eddie. (*He looks blank*) Edwin. You have to go on for him.

GEORGE: On for him.

MEG: Well he can't go on. He's been in a car accident.

GEORGE: Yes I understood that part. But what do you mean "go on for him"?

MEG: You play the part. Now I know you haven't had a chance to rehearse it exactly, but presumably you know your lines, and you've certainly seen it enough.

GEORGE: I don't understand. Do I know you?

MEG: George, we really don't have time for this kind of joshing. Half-hour. (*Exits*)

GEORGE: My name isn't George, it's . . . well, I don't know what it is, but it isn't George.

(*Enter Sarah Siddons, a glamorous actress, perhaps in a sweeping cape*)

SARAH: My God, did you hear about Eddie?

GEORGE: Yes I did.

SARAH: It's just too, too awful. Now good luck tonight, George darling, we're all counting on you. Of course, you're a little too young for the part, and you are shorter than Edwin so we'll cut all the lines about bumping your head on the ceiling. And don't forget when I cough three times, that's your cue to unzip the back of my dress and then I'll slap you. We changed it from last night. (*She starts to exit*)

GEORGE: Wait, please. What play are we doing exactly?

SARAH: (*Stares at him*) What?

GEORGE: What is the play please.

SARAH: Coward.

GEORGE: Pardon?

SARAH: Coward. (*Looks at him as if he's crazy*) It's the Coward. Noel Coward. (*Suddenly relaxing*) George, don't do that. For a second, I thought you were serious. Break a leg, darling. (*Exits*)

GEORGE: (*To himself*) Coward. I wonder if it's *Private Lives*. At least I've seen that one. I don't remember rehearsing it exactly. And am I an actor? I thought I was an accountant. And why does everyone call me George?

(*Enter Dame Ellen Terry, younger than Sarah, a bit less grand*)

ELLEN: Hello, Stanley. I heard about Edwin. Good luck tonight. We're counting on you.

GEORGE: Wait. What play are we doing?

ELLEN: Very funny, Stanley.

GEORGE: No really. I've forgotten.

ELLEN: *Checkmate.*

GEORGE: *Checkmate?*

ELLEN: By Samuel Beckett. You know, in the garbage cans. You always play these jokes, Stanley, just don't do it onstage. Well, good luck tonight. I mean, break a leg. Did you hear? Edwin broke both legs. (*Exits*)

GEORGE: I've never heard of *Checkmate*.

(*Re-enter Meg*)

MEG: George, get into costume. We have 15 minutes. (*Exits*)

(*Enter Henry Irving, age 28–33*)

HENRY: Good God, I'm late. Hi, Eddie. Oh you're not Eddie. Who are you?

GEORGE: You've never seen me before?

HENRY: Who the devil are you?

GEORGE: I don't really know. George, I think. Maybe Stanley, but probably George. I think I'm an accountant.

HENRY: Look, no one's allowed backstage before a performance. So you'll have to leave, or I'll be forced to report you to the stage manager.

GEORGE: Oh she knows I'm here already.

HENRY: Oh. Well, if Meg knows you're here it must be alright. I suppose. It's not my affair. I'm late enough already. (*Exits*)

MEG: (*Off-stage*) 10 minutes, the call is 10 minutes, everybody.

GEORGE: I better just go home. (*Takes off his pants*) Oh dear, I didn't mean to do that.

(*Enter Meg*)

MEG: George, stop that. Go into the dressing room to change. Really, you keep this up and we'll bring you up on charges.

GEORGE: But where is the dressing room?

MEG: George, you're not amusing. It's that way. And give me those. (*Takes his pants*) I'll go soak them for you.

GEORGE: Please don't soak my pants.

MEG: Don't tell me my job. Now go get changed. The call is 5 minutes. (*Pushes him off to dressing room; crosses back the other way, calling out:*) 5 minutes, everyone. 5 minutes. Places. (*Exits*)

(*A curtain closes on the stage. Darkness. Lights come up on the curtain. A voice is heard*)

VOICE: Ladies and gentlemen, may I have your attention please? At this evening's performance, the role of Elyot, normally played by Edwin Booth, will be played by George Spelvin. The role of Amanda, normally played by Sarah Bernhardt, will be played by Sarah Siddons. The role of Kitty the bar maid will be played by Mrs. Patrick Campbell. Dr. Crippin will play himself. The management wishes to remind the audience that the taking of photographs is strictly forbidden by law, and is dangerous as it may disorient the actor. Thank you.

(*The curtain opens. There is very little set, but probably a small set piece to indicate the railing of a terrace balcony. Some other set piece [a chair, a table, a cocktail bar] might be used to indicate wealth, elegance, French Riviera.*

Sarah Siddons is present when the curtain opens. She is in a glamorous evening gown, and is holding a cocktail glass and standing behind the terrace railing, staring out above the audience's head. There is the sound of applause.

After a moment George arrives onstage, fairly pushed on. He is dressed as Hamlet—black leotard and large gold medallion around his neck. [He might be missing the bottom part of the leotard and still be in his boxer shorts.] As soon as he enters, several flash photos are taken, which disorient him greatly. When he can, he looks out and sees the audience and is very taken aback.

We hear music)

SARAH: Extraordinary how potent cheap music is.

GEORGE: What?

SARAH: Extraordinary how potent cheap music is.

GEORGE: Yes, that's true. Am I supposed to be Hamlet?

SARAH: (*Alarmed; then going on*) Whose yacht do you think that is?

GEORGE: Where?

SARAH: The duke of Westminster, I expect. It always is.

GEORGE: Ah, well, perhaps. To be or not to be. I don't know any more of it.

(*She looks irritated at him; then she coughs three times. He unzips her dress, she slaps him*)

SARAH: Elyot, please. We are on our honeymoons.

GEORGE: Are we?

SARAH: Yes. (*Irritated, being over-explicit*) Me with Victor, and you with Sibyl.

GEORGE: Ah.

SARAH: Tell me about Sibyl.

GEORGE: I've never met her.

SARAH: Ah, Elyot, you're so amusing. You're married to Sibyl. Tell me about her.

GEORGE: Nothing much to tell really. She's sort of nondescript, I'd say.

SARAH: I bet you were going to say that she's just like Lady Bundle, and that she has several chins, and one blue eye and one brown eye, and a third eye in the center of her forehead. Weren't you?

GEORGE: Yes. I think so.

SARAH: Victor's like that too. (*Long pause*) I bet you were just about to tell me that you traveled around the world.

GEORGE: Yes I was. I traveled around the world.

SARAH: How was it?

GEORGE: The world?

SARAH: Yes.

GEORGE: Oh, very nice.

SARAH: I always feared the Taj Mahal would look like a biscuit box. Did it?

GEORGE: Not really.

SARAH: (*She's going to give him the cue again*) I always feared the Taj Mahal would look like a biscuit box. Did it?

GEORGE: I guess it did.

SARAH: (*Again*) I always feared the Taj Mahal would look like a biscuit box. Did it?

GEORGE: Hard to say. What brand biscuit box?

SARAH: I always feared the Taj Mahal would look like a biscuit box. Did it? (*Pause*) Did it? Did it?

GEORGE: I wonder whose yacht that is out there.

SARAH: Did it? Did it? Did it? Did it?

(*Enter Meg. She's put on an apron and maid's hat and carries a duster, but is otherwise still in her stage manager's garb*)

MEG: My, this balcony looks dusty. I think I'll just clean it up a little. (*Dusts and goes to George and whispers in his ear; exits*)

GEORGE: Not only did the Taj Mahal look like a biscuit box, but women should be struck regularly like gongs.

(*Applause*)

SARAH: Extraordinary how potent cheap music is.

GEORGE: Yes. Quite extraordinary.

SARAH: How was China?

GEORGE: China?

SARAH: You traveled around the world. How was China?

GEORGE: I liked it, but I felt homesick.

SARAH: (*Again this is happening; gives him cue again*) How was China?

GEORGE: Lots of rice. The women bind their feet.

SARAH: How was China?

GEORGE: I hated it. I missed you.

SARAH: *How was China?*

GEORGE: I hated it. I missed . . . Sibyl.

SARAH: How was China?

GEORGE: I . . . miss the maid. Oh, maid!

SARAH: How was China?

GEORGE: Just wait a moment please. Oh, maid! (*Enter Meg*) Ah, there you are. I think you missed a spot here.

(*She crosses, dusts, and whispers in his ear; exits*)

SARAH: How was China?

GEORGE: (*With authority*) Very large, China.

SARAH: And Japan?

GEORGE: (*Doesn't know, but makes a guess*) Very . . . small, Japan.

SARAH: And Ireland?

GEORGE: Very . . . green.

SARAH: And Iceland?

GEORGE: Very white.

SARAH: And Italy?

GEORGE: Very . . . Neapolitan.

SARAH: And Copenhagen?

GEORGE: Very . . . cosmopolitan.

SARAH: And Florida?

GEORGE: Very . . . condominium.

SARAH: And Perth Amboy?

GEORGE: Very . . . mobile home, I don't know.

SARAH: And Sibyl?

GEORGE: What?

SARAH: Do you love Sibyl?

GEORGE: Who's Sibyl?

SARAH: Your new wife, who you married after you and I got our divorce.

GEORGE: Oh were we married? Oh yes, I forgot that part.

SARAH: Elyot, you're so amusing. You make me laugh all the time. (*Laughs*) So, do you love Sibyl?

GEORGE: Probably. I married her.

(*Pause. She coughs three times, he unzips her dress, she slaps him*)

SARAH: Oh, Elyot, darling, I'm sorry. We were mad to have left each other. Kiss me.

(*They kiss. Enter Dame Ellen Terry as Sibyl, in an evening gown*)

ELLEN: Oh, how ghastly.

SARAH: Oh dear. And this must be Sibyl.

ELLEN: Oh how ghastly. What shall we do?

SARAH: We must all speak in very low voices and attempt to be civilized.

ELLEN: Is this Amanda? Oh, Elyot, I think she's simply obnoxious.

SARAH: How very rude.

ELLEN: Oh, Elyot, how can you treat me like this?

GEORGE: Hello, Sibyl.

ELLEN: Well, since you ask, I'm very upset. I was inside writing a letter to your mother and wanted to know how to spell apothecary.

SARAH: A-P-O-T-H-E-C-A-R-Y.

ELLEN: (*Icy*) Thank you. (*Writes it down; Sarah looks over her shoulder*)

SARAH: Don't scribble, Sibyl.

ELLEN: Did my eyes deceive me, or were you kissing my husband a moment ago?

SARAH: We must all speak in very low voices and attempt to be civilized.

ELLEN: I was speaking in a low voice.

SARAH: Yes, but I could still hear you.

ELLEN: Oh. Sorry. (*Speaks too low to be heard*)

SARAH: (*Speaks inaudibly also*)

ELLEN: (*Speaks inaudibly*)

SARAH: (*Speaks inaudibly*)

ELLEN: (*Speaks inaudibly*)

SARAH: I can't hear a bloody word she's saying. The woman's a nincompoop. Say something, Elyot.

GEORGE: I couldn't hear her either.

ELLEN: Elyot, you have to choose between us immediately—do you love this creature, or do you love me?

GEORGE: I wonder where the maid is.

ELLEN AND SARAH: (*Together, furious*) Forget about the maid, Elyot! (*They look embarrassed*)

ELLEN: You could never have a lasting relationship with a maid. Choose between the two of us.

GEORGE: I choose . . . oh God, I don't know my lines. I don't know how I got here. I wish I *weren't* here. I wish I had joined the monastery like I almost did right after high school. I almost joined, but then I didn't.

SARAH: (*Trying to cover*) Oh, Elyot, your malaria is acting up again and you're ranting. Come, come, who do you choose, me or that baggage over there.

ELLEN: You're the baggage, not I. Yes, Elyot, who do you choose?

GEORGE: I choose . . . (*To Sarah*) I'm sorry, what is your name?

SARAH: Amanda.

GEORGE: I choose Amanda. I think that's what he does in the play.

ELLEN: Very well. I can accept defeat gracefully. I don't think I'll send this letter to your mother. She has a loud voice and an overbearing manner and I don't like her taste in tea china. I hope, Elyot, that when you find me hanging from the hotel lobby chandelier with my eyes all bulged out and my tongue hanging out, that you'll be very, very sorry. Goodbye. (*Exits*)

SARAH: What a dreadful sport she is.

GEORGE: (*Doing his best to say something his character might*) Poor Sibyl. She's going to hang herself.

SARAH: Some women should be hung regularly like tapestries. Oh who cares? Whose yacht do you think that is?

GEORGE: (*Remembering*) The duke of Westminster, I exp . . .

SARAH: (*Furious*) How dare you mention that time in Mozambique? (*Slaps him*) Oh, darling, I'm sorry. (*Moving her cigarette grandly*) I love you madly!

GEORGE: (Gasps) I've inhaled your cigarette ash.

(*He coughs three times. Sarah looks confused, then unzips the front of his Hamlet doublet. He looks confused, then slaps her. She slaps him back with a vengeance. They both look confused*)

SARAH: There, we're not angry anymore, are we? Oh, Elyot, wait for me here and I'll pack my things and we'll run away together before Victor gets back. Oh, darling, isn't it extraordinary how potent cheap music can be?

(*She exits; recorded applause on her exit. George sort of follows a bit, but then turns back to face the audience. Flash photos are taken again; George blinks and is disoriented. Lights change, the sound of trumpets is heard, and Henry Irving, dressed in Shakespearean garb, enters and bows grandly to George*)

HENRY: Hail to your Lordship!

GEORGE: Oh hello. Are you Victor?

HENRY: The same, my Lord, and your poor servant ever.

GEORGE: This doesn't sound like Noel Coward.

HENRY: A truant disposition, good my Lord.

GEORGE: You're not Victor, are you?

HENRY: My Lord, I came to see your father's funeral.

GEORGE: Oh yes? And how was it?

HENRY: Indeed, my Lord, it followed hard upon.

GEORGE: Hard upon? Yes, I see. (*Enter Meg*) Oh, good, the maid. (*She whispers to him*) Thrift, thrift, Horatio. The funeral baked meats did coldly furnish forth the marriage tables. What does that mean? (*Meg exits*) Ah, she's gone already.

HENRY: My Lord, I think I saw him yesternight.

GEORGE: Did you? Who?

HENRY: My Lord, the king your father.

GEORGE: The king my father?

HENRY: Season your admiration for a while with an attent ear till I may deliver upon the witness of these gentlemen this marvel to you.

GEORGE: I see. I'm Hamlet now, right?

HENRY: Sssssh! (*Rattling this off in a very Shakespearean way:*)

> Two nights together had these gentlemen,
> Marcellus and Bernardo, on their watch
> In the dead waste and middle of the night
> Been thus encountered. A figure like your father,
> Arméd at point exactly, cap-a-pe,
> Appears before them and with solemn march
> Goes slow and stately by them. Thrice he walked
> By their oppressed and fear-surprised eyes
> Within his truncheon's length, whilst they, distilled
> Almost to jelly with the act of fear,
> Stand dumb and speak not to him. This to me
> In dreadful secrecy impart they did,
> And I with them the third night kept the watch,
> Where, as they had delivered, both in time,
> Form of the thing, each word made true and good,
> The apparition comes. I knew your father.
> These hands are not more like.

GEORGE: Oh, my turn? Most strange and wondrous tale you tell, Horatio. It doth turn my ear into a very . . . (*At a loss*) merry . . . bare bodkin.

HENRY: As I do live, my honored lord, tis true,
and we did think it writ down in our duty
To let you know of it.

GEORGE: Well, thank you very much. (*Pause*)

HENRY: Oh yes, my Lord. He wore his beaver up.

GEORGE: His beaver up. He wore his beaver up. And does he usually wear it down?

HENRY: A countenance more in sorrow than in anger.

GEORGE: Well I am sorry to hear that. My father was a king of much renown. A favorite amongst all in London town. (*Pause*) And in Denmark.

HENRY: I war'nt it will.

GEORGE: I war'nt it will also.

HENRY: Our duty to your honor. (*Exits*)

GEORGE: Where are you going? Don't go. (*Smiles out at audience*)

(*Enter Sarah dressed as Queen Gertrude*)

Oh, Amanda, good to see you. Whose yacht do you think that is?

SARAH: O Hamlet, speak no more.
Thou turn'st mine eyes into my very soul,
And there I see such black and grainéd spots
As will not leave their tinct.

GEORGE: I haven't seen Victor. Someone was here who I thought might have been him, but it wasn't.

SARAH: Oh speak to me no more.
These words like daggers enter in mine ears.
No more, sweet Hamlet.

GEORGE: Very well. What do you want to talk about?

SARAH: No more! (*Exits*)

GEORGE: Oh don't go. (*Pause; smiles uncomfortably at the audience*) Maybe someone else will come out in a minute. (*Pause*) Of course, sometimes people have soliloquies in Shakespeare. Let's just wait a moment more and maybe someone will come.

(*The lights suddenly change to a dim blue background and one bright, white spot center stage. George is not standing in the spot*)

Oh dear. (*He moves somewhat awkwardly into the spot, decides to do his best to live up to the requirements of the moment*)

To be or not to be, that is the question.
(*Doesn't know any more*) Oh maid! (*No response; remembers that actors call for "line"*) Line. Line! Ohhhh.
Oh, what a rogue and peasant slave am I.
Whether tis nobler in the mind's eye to kill oneself, or not killing oneself, to sleep a great deal.
We are such stuff as dreams are made on; and our lives are rounded by a little sleep.

(*The lights change. The spot goes out, and another one comes onstage right. George moves into it*)

Uh, thrift, thrift, Horatio. Neither a borrower nor a lender be. But to thine own self be true.
There is a special providence in the fall of a sparrow.
Extraordinary how potent cheap music can be.
Out, out, damn spot! I come to wive it wealthily in Padua; if wealthily, then happily in Padua.
(*Sings*) Brush up your Shakespeare; start quoting him now;
Da da . . .

(*Lights change again. That spot goes off; another one comes on, center stage, though closer to audience. George moves into that*)

I wonder whose yacht that is. How was China? Very large, China. How was Japan? Very small, Japan.
I pledge allegiance to the flag of the United States of America and to the republic for which it stands, one nation, under God, indivisible with liberty and justice for all.
Line! Line! Oh my God. (*Gets idea*)
O my God, I am heartily sorry for having offended thee,

and I detest all my sins because I dread the loss of heaven and the pains of hell. But most of all because they offend thee, my God, who art all good and deserving of all my love. And I resolve to confess my sins, to do penance, and to amend my life, Amen. (*Friendly*) That's the act of contrition that Catholic school children say in confession in order to be forgiven their sins. Catholic adults say it too, I imagine. I don't know any Catholic adults.

Line! (*Explaining*) When you call for a line, the stage manager normally gives you your next line, to refresh your memory.

Line!

The quality of mercy is not strained. It droppeth as the gentle rain upon the place below, when we have shuffled off this mortal coil.

Alas, poor Yorick. I knew him well. Get thee to a nunnery.

Line. Nunnery. As a child, I was taught by nuns, and then in high school I was taught by Benedictine priests. I really rather liked the nuns, they were sort of warm, though they were fairly crazy too.

Line.

I liked the priests also. The school was on the grounds of the monastery, and my junior and senior years I spent a few weekends joining in the daily routine of the monastery—prayers, then breakfast, then prayers, then lunch, then prayers, then dinner, then prayers, then sleep. I found the predictability quite attractive. And the food was good. And if there is a God, and an afterlife, and an inner life of the soul, then the monastery had everything in the proper order. And if there isn't all those things, it's still a very restful way to live.

I was going to join the monastery after high school, but they said I was too young and should wait. And then I just stopped believing in all those things, so I never did join the monastery. I became an accountant. I've studied logarithms, and cosine and tangent . . .

(*Irritated*) Line! (*Apologetic*) I'm sorry. This is supposed to be *Hamlet* or *Private Lives* or something, and I keep rattling on like a maniac. I really do apologize. I just don't recall attending a single rehearsal. I can't imagine what I was doing.

And also you came expecting to see Edwin Booth and you get me. I really am very embarrassed. Sorry. *Line!* It's a far, far better thing I do than I have ever done before. It's a far, far better place I go to than I have ever been before. (*Sings the alphabet song*) A, B, C, D, E, F, G; H, I, J, K, L, M, N, O, P; Q, R, S, T . . .

(*As he starts to sing, enter Ellen Terry, dragging two large garbage cans. She puts them side by side, gets in one*)

Oh, good. Are you Ophelia? Get thee to a nunnery.

(*She points to the other garbage can, indicating he should get in it*)

Get in? Okay. (*He does*) This must be one of those modern *Hamlets.*

(*Lights change abruptly to "Beckett lighting"*)

ELLEN: Nothing to be done. Pause. Pause. Wrinkle nose. (*Wrinkles nose*) Nothing to be done.

GEORGE: I guess you're not Ophelia.

ELLEN: We'll just wait. Pause. Either he'll come, pause pause pause, or he won't.

GEORGE: That's a reasonable attitude. Are we, on a guess, waiting for Godot?

ELLEN: No, Willie. He came already and was an awful bore. Yesterday he came. Garlic on his breath, telling a lot of unpleasant jokes about Jews and Polacks and stewardesses. He was just dreadful, pause, rolls her eyes upward. (*She rolls her eyes*)

GEORGE: Well I am sorry to hear that. Pause. So who are we waiting for?

ELLEN: We're waiting for Lefty.

GEORGE: Ah. And is he a political organizer or something, I seem to recall?

ELLEN: Yes, dear, he is a political organizer. He's always coming around saying get involved, get off your behind and organize, fight the system, do this, do that, uh, he's exhausting, he's worse than Jane Fonda. And he has garlic breath just like Godot, I don't know which of them is worse, and I hope neither of them ever comes here again. Blinks left eye, blinks right eye, closes eyes, opens them. (*Does this*)

GEORGE: So we're really not waiting for anyone, are we?

ELLEN: No, dear, we're not. It's just another happy day, pause, smile, pause, picks nit from head. (*Picks nit from head*)

GEORGE: Do you smell something?

ELLEN: That's not your line. Willie doesn't have that many lines. (*Louder*) Oh, Willie, how talkative you are this morning!

GEORGE: There seems to be some sort of muck at the bottom of this garbage can.

ELLEN: Mustn't complain, Willie. There's muck at the bottom of everyone's garbage can. Count your blessings, Willie. I do. (*Counts to herself, eyes closed*) One. Two. Three. Are you counting, Willie?

GEORGE: I guess so.

ELLEN: I'm up to three. Three is my eyesight. (*Opens her eyes*) Oh my God, I've gone blind. I can't see, Willie. Oh my God. Oh what a terrible day. Oh dear. Oh my. (*Suddenly very cheerful again*) Oh well. Not so bad really. I only used my eyes occasionally. When I wanted to see something. But no more!

GEORGE: I really don't know this play at all.

ELLEN: Count your blessings, Willie. Let me hear you count them.

GEORGE: Alright. One. Two. Three. That's my eyesight. Four. That's my hearing. Five, that's my . . . Master Charge. Six, that's . . .

ELLEN: Did you say God, Willie?

GEORGE: No.

ELLEN: Why did you leave the monastery, Willie? Was it the same reason I left the opera?

GEORGE: I have no idea.

ELLEN: I left the opera because I couldn't sing. They were mad to have hired me. Certifiable. And they were certified shortly afterward, the entire staff. They reside now at the Rigoletto Home for the Mentally Incapacitated. In Turin. Pause. Tries to touch her nose with her tongue. (*Does this*)

VOICE: Ladies and gentlemen, may I have your attention please?

ELLEN: Oh, Willie, listen. A voice. Perhaps there is a God.

VOICE: At this evening's performance, the role of Sir Thomas More, the man for all seasons, normally played by Edwin Booth, will be played by George Spelvin. The role of Lady Alice, normally played by Sarah Bernhardt, will be played by Sarah Siddons. The role of Lady Margaret, normally played by Eleonora Duse, will be read by the stage manager. And at this evening's performance the executioner will play himself.

GEORGE: What did he say?

ELLEN: The executioner will play himself.

GEORGE: What does he mean, the executioner will play himself?

(*Enter Sarah as Lady Alice [Sir Thomas More's wife] and Meg with a few costumed touches but otherwise in her stage manager's garb and carrying a script as Lady Margaret [Sir Thomas More's daughter])*

MEG: Oh father, why have they locked you up in this dreadful dungeon, it's more than I can bear.

SARAH: I've brought you a custard, Thomas.

MEG: Mother's brought you a custard, father.

GEORGE: Yes, thank you.

MEG: Oh father, if you don't give in to King Henry, they're going to cut your head off.

SARAH: Aren't you going to eat the custard I brought you, Thomas?

GEORGE: I'm not hungry, thank you.

(Sudden alarming crash of cymbals, or something similarly startling musically occurs. The Executioner appears upstage. He is dressed as the traditional headsman—the black mask, bare chest and arms, the large ax)

GEORGE: Oh my God, I've got to get out of here.

MEG: He's over here. And he'll never give in to the King.

GEORGE: No, no, I might. Quick, is this all about Anne Boleyn and everything?

MEG: Yes, and you won't give in because you believe in the Catholic Church and the infallibility of the Pope and the everlasting life of the soul.

GEORGE: I don't necessarily believe in any of that. *(To Executioner)* Oh, sir, there's been an error. I think it's fine if the King marries Anne Boleyn. I just want to wake up.

MEG: Oh don't deny God, father, just to spare our feelings. Mother and I are willing to have you dead if it's a question of principle.

SARAH: The first batch of custard didn't come out all that well, Thomas. This is the second batch. But it has a piece of hair in it, I think.

GEORGE: Oh shut up about your custard, would you? I don't think the Pope is infallible at all. I think he's a normal man with normal capabilities who wears gold slippers. I thought about joining the monastery when I was younger, but I didn't do it.

ELLEN: (*Waking up from a brief doze*) Oh I was having such a pleasant dream, Willie. Go ahead, let him cut your head off, it'll be a nice change of pace.

(*The Executioner, who has been motionless, now moves. In a sudden gesture, he reveals the cutting block that waits for George's head. Note: In the Playwrights Horizons production, our set designer constructed a square furniture piece that doubled as a settee and/or small cocktail table during the* Private Lives *section. However, when the Executioner kicked the top of it, the piece fell open, revealing itself to contain a bloodied cutting block*)

GEORGE: That blade looks very real to me. I want to wake up now. Or change plays. I wonder whose yacht that is out there. (*Sarah offers him the custard again*) No, thank you. A horse, a horse! My kingdom for a horse!

EXECUTIONER: Sir Thomas More, you have been found guilty of the charge of High Treason. The sentence of the court is that you be taken to the Tower of London, thence to the place of execution, and there your head shall be stricken from your body, and may God have mercy on your soul.

(*Meg helps George out of the garbage can*)

GEORGE: All this talk about God. Alright, I'm sorry I didn't join the monastery, maybe I should have, and I'm sorry I giggled during Mass in third grade, but I see no reason to be killed for it.

ELLEN: Nothing to be done. That's what I find so wonderful.

(*Meg puts George's head on the block*)

GEORGE: No!

EXECUTIONER: Do I understand you right? You wish to reverse your previous stand on King Henry's marriage to Anne and to deny the Bishop of Rome?

GEORGE: Yes, yes, God, yes. I could care less. Let him marry eight wives.

EXECUTIONER: That's a terrible legacy of cowardice for Sir Thomas More to leave behind.

GEORGE: I don't care.

EXECUTIONER: I'm going to ignore what you've said and cut your head off anyway, and then we'll all pretend you went to your death nobly. The Church needs its saints, and school children have got to have heroes to look up to, don't you all agree?

ELLEN: I agree. I know I need someone to look up to. Pause smile picks her nose. (*Does this*)

GEORGE: Yes, yes, I can feel myself waking up now. The covers have fallen off the bed, and I'm cold, and I'm going to wake up so that I can reach down and pull them up again.

EXECUTIONER: Sir Thomas, prepare to meet your death.

GEORGE: Be quiet, I'm about to wake up.

EXECUTIONER: Sir Thomas, prepare to meet your death.

GEORGE: I'm awake! (*Looks around him; Sarah offers him custard again*) No, I'm not.

SARAH: He doesn't know his lines.

EXECUTIONER: Sir Thomas, prepare to meet your death.

GEORGE: Line! Line!

MEG: You turn to the executioner and say, "Friend, be not afraid of your office. You send me to God."

GEORGE: I don't like that line. Give me another.

MEG: That's the line in the script, George. Say it.

GEORGE: I don't want to.

MEG: Say it.

ELLEN: Say it, Willie. It'll mean a lot to me and to generations of school children to come.

SARAH: O Hamlet, speak the speech, I pray you, trippingly
on the tongue.

EXECUTIONER: Say it!

GEORGE: Friend, be not afraid of your office. You send me
. . . Extraordinary how potent cheap music is.

MEG: That's not the line.

GEORGE: Women should be struck regularly like gongs.

MEG: George, say the line right.

GEORGE: They say you can never dream your own death, so
I expect I'll wake up just as soon as he starts to bring the
blade down. So perhaps I should get it over with.

MEG: Say the proper line, George.

GEORGE: Friend, be not afraid of your office.

ELLEN: Goodbye, Willie.

SARAH: Goodbye, Hamlet.

MEG: Goodbye, George.

EXECUTIONER: Goodbye, Sir Thomas.

GEORGE: You send me to God.

(*Executioner raises the ax to bring it down. Blackout.
Sound of the ax coming down*)

EXECUTIONER: (*In darkness*) Behold the head of Sir Thomas
More.

ELLEN: (*In darkness*) Oh I wish I weren't blind and could
see that, Willie. Oh well, no matter. It's still been another

happy day. Pause, smile, wrinkles nose, pause, picks nit from head, pause, pause, wiggles ears, all in darkness, utterly useless, no one can see her. She stares ahead. Count two. End of play.

(*Music plays. Maybe canned applause. Lights come up for curtain calls. The four take their bows [if Henry Irving does not play the executioner, he comes out for his bow as well]. Sarah and Ellen have fairly elaborate bows, perhaps receiving flowers from the executioner. They gesture for George to take his bow, but he seems to be dead. They applaud him, and then bow again, and lights out*)